P9-CDC-634

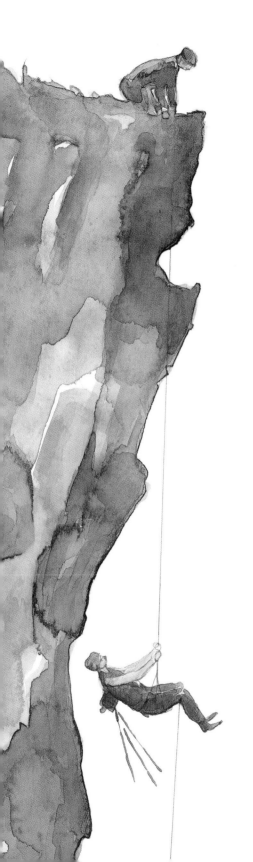

In the Belly of an Ox

The Unexpected Photographic Adventures
of Richard and Cherry Kearton

Written and illustrated by **Rebecca Bond**

Houghton Mifflin Books for Children
HOUGHTON MIFFLIN HARCOURT
Boston New York 2009

While London streets bustled
with carriages and trolleys,
and great talk
of steam-trains! and telephones!
and new electric lights as bright as day . . .

two boys—Richard and Cherry Kearton—
were born on a farm in Yorkshire.
They were two of five children,
and they were nine years apart.

As small boys, they attended school in a nearby village.

As young lads, they tended sheep in moorland pastures.
And all the while, among and between the hills of Yorkshire,
they spent their childhoods deliberately discovering.

They especially marveled at the architecture
of living things:

The structure of nests.

The lattice of webs.

The shapes of prints.

The patterns of play.

The camouflage of nature.

The designs of flight.

Richard and Cherry spent their boyhood years outside,
on that thin line where wide land meets huge sky.

Everywhere they looked, they saw something to solve.
For two boys in the hills of Yorkshire,
it was a time of magical discovery.

But like all children, the brothers grew up.
Richard left for work in London.
He had been offered a job at Cassell Publishing House.

Four years later,
when their father died,
fifteen-year-old Cherry left for London too.
He would work at Cassell alongside his brother.

They had traded the stretch of Yorkshire fields
for the crush of London streets.

And though London was noisy with new construction,
crackled with big ideas, and was alive with people,
Richard and Cherry were lonesome for the moorlands.
For company, Richard opened the windows of his small
city apartment to stray cats.

On weekends, any chance they got,
they visited friends in the country.

One weekend, for fun, Cherry bought along his new
camera and took a photograph of a thrush's nest.

It was a perfect image of the real and beautiful nest.
No one they knew had ever taken a picture like this before.
Seeing his brother's photograph,
Richard had an ambitious idea.

He puzzled over how to pull it off.
They would have to be sneaky and clever.

They set to their challenge with a great will.
They couldn't give up their jobs,
but they did give up some sleep.
They rose at three or four in the
mornings and left London before the
city was awake.

They crept about under hedgerows,
among reeds and rushes,
between brambles and briars,
and into the branches of trees.

By nine a.m., they were back in London
at Cassell Publishing House,
at their desks, working.

These early spring mornings and long spring
weekends brought the brothers some success,
but soon they realized the challenge they'd invented
was bigger still.
They needed veils, and disguises.

First, they sewed together two great blankets, back to
back. One side cloaked Cherry in dry-grass yellow.

The other hid him in lush spring green.

It worked!
The brothers grew more excited.

Soon Richard and Cherry were talking about
better ways to disappear.
They began to design "hides."

These took a while to set up.
Richard had to tuck Cherry
and his camera in.

But once Cherry was concealed
inside a wagon,
beneath a frame and a canvas,
under a heap of hay,
the swallows never knew Cherry existed.

Likewise, enclosed inside
an old "tree trunk"
made with poles and cloth

and layered with leaves,
Cherry was as good as invisible
to the thrushes and nuthatches
with their nests full of eggs.

And crouched within the belly of an ox—a hollow ox made from a real bullock hide stretched over a light wooden frame—Cherry all but vanished entirely.

Just as the Greeks had hidden from the Trojans inside the belly of a horse, Richard and Cherry reasoned they too might hide from birds in the belly of an ox. They asked a well-known taxidermist in Piccadilly to build them one.

Inside it was cramped, hot and smelly, but it was an ingenious way to photograph the nests of magpies and partridges, larks and quail, without scaring away the mother birds.

Still, their ox was not perfect.
When a windstorm blew the ox over,
and Cherry with it,
Cherry waited an hour,
six legs in the air,
for Richard's rescue.

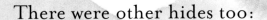
There were other hides too:

A great rock hide, made from five walls,
held together with hooks and designed
from artificial materials
to look like limestone—

just the thing for disappearing
on stony hillsides,
where curlews liked to nest.

A stuffed sheep hide, with their camera
arranged inside. Cherry could take his
pictures with a pneumatic tube (air
squeezed through the hose triggered the
shutter) from a safe distance away.

And even a tree-trunk mask,
made from an old stump,
hollowed with a chisel and a mallet.
Once it was covered in foliage,
Cherry could wear his mask in the fields
and not be seen for hours.

Richard and Cherry captured each of
the images they sought, one by one.
Now again was a time of magical
discovery for the brothers.

Some surely thought the Kearton brothers foolhardy
for enduring hunger and thirst,
insect stings and rainstorms.

For lugging their heavy equipment all around Britain,
more than 30,000 miles, by railroad and steamboat
and often by foot.

For sleeping wherever they could:
in old ruins, or outside in plain air.

Not to mention
wading through bogs,
roping down precipitous cliffs,
and climbing into the branches of impossibly tall trees,
simply for a photograph!

But Richard and Cherry were doing
just exactly what they loved.

It took them three years.

By the time they were finished,
Richard and Cherry had accomplished something
no one ever had before.
They created the first nature book ever
entirely illustrated with photographs.
They called it *British Birds' Nests*.
Cassell published it in the fall of 1895.

It included the eggs and nests of every bird they knew:
bitterns and blackbirds,
corn buntings and spotted crakes,
crossbills and curlews and dippers,
skylarks and snipes,
swifts and wrens.

It depicted hundreds of nests, eggs, and birds
in their natural surroundings
so anyone might know and name them
and love them
as the brothers did.

Dr. Bowdler Sharpe of the London Natural History Museum
declared that the book "marked a new era in natural history."

All of a sudden, because of *British Birds' Nests*,
in the country and cities and reaches beyond,
people were out looking for birds and their nests.

And instead of stealing the nests,
or even plundering them for their egg trophies,
curious observers were now content
to identify the nests and eggs and birds
and to leave the eggs in their nests to hatch.

One reader wrote, "I consider that the birds ought to be
extremely grateful to you for inventing bird-photography."

And though Richard and Cherry Kearton each would
go on to do more remarkable things
in natural history, and to live full, inspired lives,
nothing was ever more important to the brothers
than this first shared book.

Richard and Cherry Kearton
had gathered in one place
a gallery
of every bird they loved.

Hollow sheep, with camera inside

Moorhen nest

Common curlew nest

Jackdaw nest

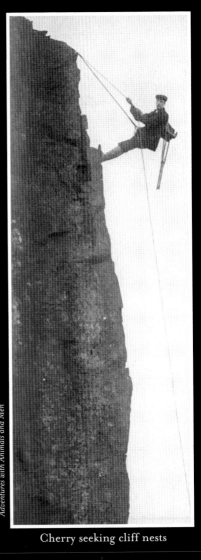

With Nature and a Camera

Cherry photographing in river

Adventures with Animals and Men

Cherry seeking cliff nests

Wild Life at Home

Cherry climbing tree with camera on back

British Birds' Nests

Sedge warbler nest

For David Walton, for giving me the visual world I love

www.hmhbooks.com

Houghton Mifflin Books for Children is an imprint of Houghton Mifflin Harcourt Publishing Company.

The text of this book is set in Mrs. Eaves Bold.
The illustrations are watercolor and pen and ink.

Library of Congress Cataloging-in-Publication Data is on file.

ISBN: 978-0-547-07675-1

Printed in Singapore
TWP 10 9 8 7 6 5 4 3 2 1

SOURCES

BIBLIOGRAPHY

Kearton, Cherry. *Adventures with Animals and Men*. London: Longmans, Green and Company, 1935.
——. *Photographing Wild Life Across the World*. London: J. W. Arrowsmith, 1913.
Kearton, Richard. *Birds' Nests, Eggs, and Egg-Collecting*. London: Cassell & Company, 1895.
——. *British Birds' Nests: How, Where, and When to Find and Identify Them*. London: Cassell & Company, 1895.
——. *Wild Bird Adventures*. 1923.
——. *Wild Life at Home*. 1907.
——. *With Nature and a Camera*. London: Cassell & Company, 1898.
Mitchell, W. R. *Watch the Birdie: The Life and Times of Richard and Cherry Kearton, Pioneers of Nature Photography*. Giggleswick, United Kingdom: Castleberg, 2001.

QUOTES

"Dr. Bowlder Sharpe . . ." Kearton, *British Birds' Nests*, p. v.
"I consider the birds ought . . ." Kearton, *British Birds' Nests*, p. vii.
"I doubt not we shall be . . ." Kearton, *With Nature and a Camera*, p. x.
"I fixed a rope . . ." Kearton, *Photographing Wild Life Across the World*, p. 268.
"I knew him to get up . . ." Mitchell, *Watch the Birdie*, p. 112.
"There are some people . . ." Kearton, *Adventures with Animals and Men*, p. 1.

Adventures with Animals and Men

Cherry standing on Richard's shoulders to get close to a nest

There are some people—and I myself am one of them—who are represented by pegs of such irregular shape that neither a square hole nor a round one will ever accommodate itself to them. For such people life can carry little happiness except in the rare instances when they are able to carve out an entirely new-shaped hole, never before thought of, but exactly fitting their peculiarities. Fortunately for myself, I was able to do that.

— Cherry Kearton (1871–1940)

I doubt not we shall be accused of adventurous foolhardiness.

—Richard Kearton (1862–1928)

Cherry's Later Life

CHERRY ONLY BECAME MORE ADVENTUROUS. He traveled around the world photographing wild animals—lions and hippopotamuses, bears and rhinoceroses. He continued to devise ingenious ways to photograph them.

In India, while photographing tigers, Cherry tied himself into his tree perch at night. "I fixed a rope around my chest and made it fast," he said, "so that if I went to sleep, I should not tumble out."

Throughout his life, Cherry always had great conviction that photography methods should be used for the protection and appreciation of wildlife and should not be used in conjunction with hunting for animal trophies.

Cherry married and had two children. He would continue to travel the world in pursuit of animal adventure until his death in 1940.

Richard's Later Life

RICHARD TOO CONTINUED TO TRAVEL, though not as widely as his brother. He preferred to stay at home in Britain, to study and to photograph and to write. He never stopped looking for nests, and he found some extraordinary ones, such as a robin's nest built into the bookcase of a girls' school in Reading. The nest was lined with varied tints of hair from all the girls who lived there.

Richard wrote or contributed to twenty books. He felt it was his job to share what he had discovered and to make himself available to anyone who needed his advice.

After he married and had five children, his daughter Grace would say of Richard, "I knew him to get up one night in the middle of a heavy rainstorm to walk down a long garden to a thrush nest. He took with him an old trilby hat and used it to cover the nest. Next morning he had the joy of finding mother bird and her young quite dry under the old hat."

Richard's greatest hope was to send young naturalists into the field after him. There is no doubt he did that. He lived until 1928.